# Changing Your Reality

I0181720

*Gerald Seals II*

**Empowering Life Publishing**
*Signature Series*: **Wisdom & Vibe Brand**

WISDOM & VIBE BRAND

Unless otherwise indicated, all scriptural quotations are from the King James Version of the Bible.

Changing Your Reality
Published by: Empowering Life International
Gerald Seals II, dba Wisdom & Vibe Brand, LLC
1209 Dayton Yellow Springs Rd. #299
Fairborn, Ohio 45324
ISBN  978-0692237694

Printed and distributed by Empowering Life International, Inc.

# Contents

*Dedication*
*Special Thanks*
*Forward*
*Introduction*

## Chapter

# Dedication

As always, I remain appreciative of the Most High wisdom and forgiveness. It's your Divine Spirit that give me divine guidance, wisdom, knowledge and understanding, which assist me to pursue a daily transformation and enlightenment.

To my lover, companion, best friend, consoler and partner in life my wife, Latrease L. Seals.

To my children Gerald, Shalom and Jalissa your generation shares the responsibility to help individuals make personal change obtainable.

I also dedicate this message unto those that observe and believe in the principles of *Changing Your Reality* and also unto the emerging and unborn generations.

# Special Thanks

To all those that have been patronizing our works and vision we can not fulfill it without you.

To Gloria Hunter, thank you for your editorial assistance.

To all the ministries, community groups, symposiums, community groups, colleges and any assembly that has allowed me to share what is in my heart.

To our Personal Distributors (Wisdom Ground Team), thank you for continuing to sell our wisdom books unto your family, friends and associates.

To all my brotha's and sista's who have been true friends, partners and a strength unto me, I truly thank all of you.

To all the people and communities that are striving to implement these spiritual principles.

Peace, Love and Blessing upon you all!

# Foreword

Why Change?  What is the importance of change?  What is my reality?  As I travel and speak across the country, I am often puzzled by people who do not perceive the importance of change or the need to change.  As a Christian, I was always taught that the life of a believer is the process of continuous change and that the spiritual journey is a road of ongoing transformation.  Even the process of salvation is more than just accepting Jesus as Lord and personal Savior; it is a mental process of renovating my thoughts so that my thoughts became the thoughts of the creator of the universe.  I understood that not only did I have the ability to change but I also had the ability to change my reality.  The book, *Changing Your Reality* captures this powerful concept.  *Changing Your Reality* is the blueprint to redesigning your mental mindset – change your mind, change your reality.

Author, Gerald Seals, through this meditative and thought provoking book provides hope in a world calling for change.  This is not a book for the meek or the mild mannered. Its purpose and design is to give the reader an insightful foundation to change his or her environment.  If these principals are applied, the reader will not only transform themselves they will have the ability to change their legacy and impact future generations.  They will have the ability to change their reality.

Having had the privilege of knowing Gerald as both a fellow author, business partner and a friend, I know him to be a catalyst of change. We are kindred spirits who are joined is a fraternal order designed to change the world as part of Empowering Life International. This book is not just a product of Empowering Life; it is a part of the cornerstone of the E.L.I movement, whose mission is to *"To improve the quality life of every person every day, through the use of training, coaching, consulting, publishing and motivation."* We at E.L.I strive to live up to our vision which is to see personal and organizational innovations that bring about improvements within the lives of individuals and organizations. Our vision is to establish a network of charter businesses, schools, and organizations that use our training, consulting, and motivational strategies and materials. We seek to advocate personal and social elevation through empowerment – economically, intellectually, spiritually and politically. We endeavor to create community development and urban renewal by empowering organizations and individuals to serve as vanguards within communities. By providing conferences, workshops, and training manuals for both the individual and organizations, Empowering Life, Inc. desires to be instrumental in the reinventing of individuals, transforming homes and communities, and creating a foundation for emerging generations to progress spiritually, socially, economically, communally, intellectually, domestically, and politically.

Gerald Seals is not only an author, but the Wisdom and Vibe Brand is an intricate part of the Empowering Life movement. His gift of synergistic leadership and vision is what helps make Empowering Life International the innovative and transformational company of the new millennium. His new book, Changing Your Reality, will help transform you and give you the tools to reinvent yourself by changing your reality.

# Introduction

*Changing Your Reality* means to change the mental image. This book provides hope to those that feel that he/she is a product from their environment. If an individual doesn't understand that he/she don't have to be a product from his/her environment, he/she will then become a product of it. If individuals embrace these principles and insights concerning changing the mental image, then change will occur among individuals, families, communities and society. Therefore, the hope that this message project is that changing the mental image is possible.

When someone does not understand the principles concerning changing the mental image, he/she will become confined into a reality that he/she aren't comfortable with. The principles within this book truly provide a key for unlocking the confinements within your mind. These principles not only unlock the confinements within your mind but it also provides a blueprint to perceive your life differently. Life is about change, which causes individuals to become dissatisfied with non-productive realities that are not beneficial for their spiritual-psycho-socio-cultural development.

You change realities through changing the thinking. As one's thinking changes, the behavior will change. Once the behavior has changed, then the social interactions will change. This is exactly what this message will do once it is implemented within someone life. Therefore, as you absorb this message and as it benefits you be sure to transfer this knowledge to your children, grandchildren and associates.

"The one who understands how to change perceptions (mental images) not only can change themselves, but they also have power to change those they influence."

*By Gerald Seals II of Wisdom & Vibe Brand*

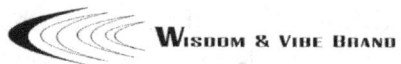

WISDOM & VIBE BRAND

# Chapter 1
# "The Beginning Factor for Mind Renewal"

*"Every visible activity begins within the mind first."*

**Proverbs 13:25**
> **The righteous eateth to the satisfying of his soul.**

**Proverbs 3:5**
> **Trust in the Lord with all thine heart; and lean not unto thine own understanding.**

The first factor for mind renewal is to have an individual craving or desire to entertain or assimilate things that will sustain the soul. Mind renewal begins with the personal desire to change the mind.

Mind renewal begins when an individual's inward man is dependent or relies on the Spirit of God. Mind renewal is based on the process of subjecting yourself to the culture of God. The goal to mind renewal is to have your spirit and mind subject to the Spirit of God, which creates oneness with God. You become subject to the Spirit of God once you understand the attributes of the Spirit of God. The attributes of the Spirit of God are *knowledge, wisdom, understanding, truth, love, peace, forgiveness, righteousness, patience* and virtuous dispositions of such. By understanding the attributes of the Spirit of God, you can then understand how to discern when the activity of the Spirit of God is being displayed or operative. For example, say you have a desire to establish a business and because of that desire the Spirit of God influence individuals that are *knowledgeable* of the process of going into business around you. According to this example revealed how the activity of the Spirit of God was being operative along with your desire to go into business, in which the Spirit of God has caused you to be around people with knowledge and knowledge is an attribute of the Spirit of God. Therefore, when you are around the attributes of the Spirit of God makes evidence that the activity of the Spirit of God is assisting the desire or ambition that you decide to carry out.

*Requirements to bring the spirit and mind subject to the Spirit of God:*

- Must not be dependent on how you view or comprehend life that doesn't correspond with the culture of God (emphasizing knowing the social, economical, domestic & political cultures that reflect universal principles)
- Must not be dependent on your practiced principles or rules for living that aren't compliant with spiritual laws
- Must not be dependent on how this social system (world) has spiritually and psychologically directed your perspective for living
- Must not be dependent on information that doesn't benefit your spirit and soul
- Must not be dependent on your personal decision-making procedures that are exempt from spiritual wisdom, knowledge and understanding

*"According to how someone understands determines how they manipulate their environment."*

The insight of this quote means we construct our life based on the understanding we have. Therefore, your life changes according to the understanding you operate from, or your life conforms to the understanding you have. The purpose of not leaning towards your own understanding is to position you to receive God's view for living life.

*"You cannot renew the mind if it is not conforming to something new."*

The base to mind renewal is to become willing to **unlearn in order to learn**. Learning is the process of fixing ideas and then making it material. Concerning spiritual development, fixed ideas can serve as a barrier for one to become more relational with the Spirit of God. Unlearning refers to looking at things from an opposite view to the point when you can see both views clearly as the other. Unlearning in order to learn is a concept that refers to an individual willing to see past his/her personal fixed ideas in order to see life from a different perspective. The concept of renewing the mind is to be willing to go through the process of undoctrinating yourself, re-indoctrinating yourself, re-instructing yourself, being open to be retrained or re-educated by a source of wisdom, knowledge, and understanding that is higher than what your previous learning has been.

*"When you are willing to unlearn in order to learn you allow yourself to rethink your existence of life and develop a different view of life."*

**James 1:22-24**
       **Be ye doers of the word, and not hearers only, deceiving your own selves.  V. 23 For if any be a hearer of the word, and not a doer, he is like unto a man beholding his natural face in a glass:  V. 24 For he beholdeth himself, and goeth his way, and straightway forgetteth what manner of man he was.**

       Mind renewal is based on coming to the place to practice and perform what you have learned.  You can't begin to change the mind until you are able to *see yourself.*  When you are able to see yourself, then you are able to renew the mind because you are able to distinguish things that will hinder the mind's renewal process or your spiritual development.

*"You can't change if you can't see differently."*

*"In order to change your thinking, you must recognize that your present thinking system is ineffective in order to develop a new thinking system."*

# Chapter 2
## "Changing Your Reality"

**James 1:23-24**
**For if any man be a hearer of the word, and not a doer, he is like unto a man beholding his natural face in a glass: V. 24 For he beholdeth himself, and goeth his way, and straightway forgetteth what manner of man he was.**

Reality refers to perception and how individuals perceive themselves, relationships, community, society and life as a whole. Perception determines what an individual will express and experience within his/her life. Change corresponds or relates to you seeing differently. In order to see differently, you must think differently. Therefore, in order to change one's thinking, one must recognize that his/her present thinking system is ineffective in order to develop a new thinking system. Shifting your reality is dependent on thinking differently.

**Proverbs 23:7**
**For as he thinketh in his heart, so is he:**

The heart changes as your thinking changes. Every action and activity you present in life began within your heart first. You cannot be what is not within your heart. What is in your heart determines what you will do and everything you do reflects your heart. Your behavior, conduct, attitude and character reveal the history of your heart. Your thinking is not separate from you and you are what you think. The people you associate with, environments or activities you attract, and the things you personally express or demonstrate are a reflection of yourself. *"So is he"*, refers to your existence, which is defined as the continual repeated cycles and visible activities or conditions in your life.

> *"The way to change your existence is to change your thinking."*
> *"The things you continue to do reveal where your heart is."*

A thought is an idea or a pattern of ideas. The process of turning something into the mind by the process of arranging ideas in a consistent pattern also defines a thought. Thinking is the power of reasoning, conceiving ideas, having the ability to organize ideas and create mental images. Thinking is an established belief system, words, opinions, values, perspectives and principles that circulate within the mind. Thinking serves as a blueprint for what a person plans to achieve or express within his/her life. Therefore, the condition of the heart determines how an individual will perceive himself/herself, his/her relationships, community and life as a whole.

> *"What you continue to experience in your life is a reflection of your thinking."*

**Matthew 6:21**

**For where your treasure is, there will your heart be also.**

The heart is programmable by the things it entertains, pleasures, values, and by what its motives and desires are. The atrocity or danger to this truth is that if an individual does not see or understand himself/herself means spirits, individuals, or society can determine what his/her existence will be. Therefore, when you don't understand or see yourself means spirits, individuals, or society can predetermine what you will do, how you will think, and also how you will behave. When someone controls an individual's thinking, the controller determines the motivations, ambitions, opinions, philosophy of living and lusts, which means that individual produces what the controller wants.

*"When someone can mold or indoctrinate your thinking, he/she doesn't have to physically force you to do anything because the one that molds or indoctrinate the mind is the one that controls the conduct of an individual."*

# Chapter 3
## "Changing Your Reality with Knowledge"

**Matthew 6:21**
**For where your treasure is, there will your heart be also.**

**Proverbs 19:2**
**Also, that the soul be without knowledge, it is not good**

What you continue to experience in your life is a reflection of your thinking. When someone can seize your heart, it means he/she can govern your life. Treasure refers to the things you entertain, value and the standards you embrace. Understanding what treasure refers to can bring an understanding to this statement, *"when someone can mold or indoctrinate your thinking, he/she don't have to physically force you to do anything because the one that molds or indoctrinate the mind is the one that controls the conduct of an individual"*. When your thinking begins to change, then your personal reality will change.

Inward transformation and changing your reality can't occur without receiving knowledge (also includes spiritual knowledge). Knowledge is truth and facts that lead someone to believe; it is available techniques and skills that can be utilized, it is principles, formulas, methods and information that is designed to bring awareness to the soul and spirit. The knowledge you've received determines the reality your soul will experience.

Knowledge is awareness.  As a soul receives knowledge, it enables it to become more sensitive or alert of the things that the soul hasn't known.  The importance of knowledge pertaining to changing your reality is that it sharpens the mental faculties.  Therefore, knowledge enhances a soul's perception.  As the soul becomes more perceptive due to receiving knowledge, the soul will become responsive towards issues, conditions or activities that effect or influence a soul development.  Knowledge causes your reality to change because it enables or encourages a soul to attempt to reach a truth.  Once the soul receives a truth, it becomes empowered to arrive to a decision by balancing conflicting opinions, information and ideologies.  Knowledge is beneficial because as a soul receives it, your behavior and thinking will change; but knowledge also can be detrimental, which is dependent on how it is used.

*"Knowledge is awareness."*

The importance knowledge serves concerning changing your reality is that it develops an awareness; and through awareness, intelligence can be developed.  Intelligence is the ability to apply knowledge to manipulate your environment or existence.  A soul without knowledge or information is not a healthy soul.  An unhealthy soul is a soul filled with anxiety, fear and hatred.  A soul without knowledge or information is not a complete soul.  The soul that is not complete is a soul divided against itself, lacks courage, lacks purpose, and lacks vision.

A soul is not valuable when it is absent of knowledge or information. The term *"good"* within the Hebrew is referred to as **property.** Therefore, a soul without knowledge or information is not its own property in the areas where it is absent of knowledge.

*"Without knowledge, you can be owned or become the property of someone else."*

*"A soul with knowledge is at an advantage."*

*"Knowledge activates intelligence."*

**Isaiah 5:13**
> **Therefore my people are gone into captivity, because they have no knowledge.**

When a soul is absent of knowledge, has been misinformed or has been victimized by propaganda, the soul can be in captivity to what it doesn't know. Captivity means to be confined or it refers to being in a realm of limitations. This means individuals can gain control of souls (people) according to the misinformation, propaganda and deprivation of knowledge that is incurred upon the victim. Knowledge either expands your limits of opportunity in life or it contracts your opportunity in life. Without knowledge, someone can gain control or an advantage over you. Without spiritual knowledge, someone can own your soul. When you do not possess spiritual knowledge for living, you will become a prisoner of the negativity in life. Human development depends on the basis of information that you has received. Without knowledge you are ill equipped to develop psychologically and spiritually.

*"Human development depends on the basis of the information that one has received."*

*"Without knowledge, you are ill equipped to develop psychologically and spiritually."*

*"A soul becomes the type of knowledge or information it has received."*

*"When you do not possess spiritual knowledge for living, you will become a prisoner of the negativity in life"*

# Chapter 4
## "Changing Your Reality with Wisdom"

**Proverbs 19:8**
**He that getteth wisdom loveth his own soul: he that keepeth understanding shall find good.**

*"Knowledge is awareness but wisdom is insight."*
*"Knowledge is power but wisdom is control."*

Wisdom is a contributing factor for changing your reality. Since wisdom is insight, it allows you to understand that a reality will change if an individual receives or develops insight. An important element for changing your reality is to *love your own soul*. To love your own soul is to acquire wisdom. As stated, *"knowledge is power but wisdom is control"* predicates that *loving your own soul* means to have a willingness to regain control over what you will express or demonstrate in your life by having your soul governed by spiritual laws or principles. Therefore, *loving your own soul* is the personal pursuit of desiring to align and subject yourself to insights that are influenced by spiritual laws or principles. *"Wisdom is insight"* confers that wisdom enables a soul to differentiate between diverse hidden motives and deceptive influences that effects the soul.

Insight is a spiritual enablement that allows you to see what is not evident to the average soul or it is the ability to comprehend the obscurity of an individual's motives and character. A Greek term "phronesis" defines wisdom as having a moral and intellectual insight. Intellect refers to the way of thinking, perspective, ideology, morale (defined as understanding the moods of people cooperating) and the attitude of an individual. Moral refers to a value system and principles of conduct.

Therefore, bringing an avouchment of definition concerning the term wisdom, you can summarize wisdom as a spiritual ability of utilizing knowledge and spiritual discernment to engineer or orchestrate the expressed nature or spirit within individuals and environments. Interpreting what wisdom is allows you to understand that wisdom is measured by what is created or produced within someone human relations. Remember *loving your own soul* refers to the desire of regaining control over what you will express or demonstrate in your life by having your soul governed by spiritual laws or principles. As an individual regains control over his/her expression will eventually effect his/her relationships, which will then influence an individual's reality or perception.

Human relations refer to how souls correspond or treat one another, which determine the social expression within a soul life. Problems or solutions, arising from organizational and interpersonal activities also refers to human relations. The content of human relations will manifest or reveal itself through souls being cooperative or confrontational. The indicators that will determine whether the human relations will reveal being cooperative or confrontational is by how souls respect and agree with one another.

Human relations can be measured according to how souls consider each other, trust one another, how devout they are, and how they value things, resources or people. The activities of interacting around others' opinions and ideas also determine what the human relations will manifest. These descriptive measurements will determine the content of the Spirit of Wisdom that is being displayed within the human relations.

The Spirit of Wisdom can be either earthy or spiritual. Earthy wisdom supports anti-social and misanthropic environments. Earthy wisdom or insight demonstrates certain dispositions within the human relations namely:

- Witnessing individuals being quarrelsome
- Witnessing individuals having pleasure in harassing one another
- Witnessing individuals diverting or realigning individuals to be indifferent to peaceful, righteous, positive and virtuous environments
- Have environment that promote or encourage one to forfeit righteousness and Godly integrity
- Have environments that create physical and mental strains on individuals
- Have detained economies
- Witnessing individuals competing for superiority over one another
- War-oriented and have warmongering mentalities.

As these diverse dispositions are operating, they will cause the human relations to lack social order and be destructive. Spiritual wisdom supports sociable and philanthropic environments. Spiritual wisdom or insight demonstrates certain dispositions within the human relations namely:

- Witnessing individuals being intelligent and having comprehensibility, which causes individuals to be straightforward with one another
- Social settings operating in simplicity instead of complexity, in other *words* being absent of propaganda, manipulation and deception
- Witnessing individuals possessing the ability to project light within their character
- Witnessing individuals having harmony within their personal relations
- Witnessing individuals being free from oppressive thoughts
- Witnessing individuals craving tranquility
- Witnessing individuals being pleasant and at ease in conversing with one another
- Prosperous economies
- Witnessing individuals not displaying false appearances of righteousness.

As these dispositions operate, the human relations will increase social order and productivity. The reason why wisdom has a significant role in changing your reality is because it affects the human relations or the lively expressions. What souls demonstrate and how they interact effects your reality because these activities influence what an individual's opinions, ideas and thoughts will be. Your opinions, ideas and thoughts will determine what you will do because the mindset determines the conduct.

The importance of having wisdom is that it allows you to see into an individual, community, people or society thinking, character, perspective, attitude, value system and principles of conduct. By having wisdom, you can make decisions based on seeing into someone's thinking, character, perception, attitude, value system and principles of conduct. As an individual has insight, those individuals can then transition his/her decisions to benefit his/her human relations.

For example, if an individual were violent, a person with wisdom would see into his/her revengeful and wrathful attitude, which allows the person with wisdom to approach or interact with the violent individual reasonably. To further expound, since the person with wisdom had access to see into the violent person's revengeful and wrathful attitude, he or she would strive not to appeal to what may be offensive, which will allow the person with wisdom and the violent person to interact harmoniously. This is how wisdom affects the human relations.

According to this example, you'll notice a violent individual, which indicates that there is knowledge of the individual (refers to knowing the condition) without having wisdom of that individual (refers to not knowing the cause of the condition). Wisdom came into the picture when the wise person discerned the revengeful and wrathful attitude. Because the person with wisdom had wisdom, it allowed him or her to *see beyond the visible condition (awareness)* and *into what causes the violent person's actions (insight)*. The wise person was able to avert a violent expression to a peaceful expression because he/she knew not to entertain what may cause the violent person to be violent. Therefore, you affect human relations by knowing how to respond to individuals' thinking, character, perception and attitude, which confirm that wisdom is *control*. Having wisdom or insight enables an individual or people to engineer what will be manifested within the environment.

# Chapter 5
# "Changing Your Reality with Understanding"

Job 28:28
### To depart from evil is understanding.

Having an understanding is an ingredient that is required in order to change your reality. According to spiritual principles, understanding is defined as the *ability* to depart from evil. This also means you measure someone level of understanding by his/her ability to deviate from the perspectives, ideologies, attitudes and characteristics of evil. Understanding is the ability to deviate or not conform to expressions of:

- Activities that harm the reputation of someone
- Corrupt acts or practices
- Social contexts supporting discomfort or repulsion
- Sorrow, distress and calamity
- Exciting bitter feelings
- Environments being intractable
- Lacking civility or graciousness
- Activities that lower the esteem of individuals and communities
- Environments that aren't advancing or developing

Once the soul has been exposed to evil and accepts it as evil, then you can have understanding. Until evil becomes a reality, the soul can remain imprisoned to evil. This means the soul's reality cannot expand out of evil because it is kept within the limits of evil due to the soul remaining unconsciously or consciously in agreement or harmony with evil. The soul maintains its agreement or harmony with evil because the soul patterns or acts in accordance with the prevailing standards or customs of evil. In other words, when evil is not a reality, the soul becomes identical or twinned with the expressions of evil. Therefore, it is imperative for a soul to be exposed of evil because it frees the *will*. When the soul's *will* isn't free, it will eventually become weakened; and when the *will* is weakened, a dependent mentality develops. As the mind is in a dependent state, it will consciously accept more evil realities because the "*will*" will lose its desire to differentiate the good from evil.

> *"When the soul remains subject to evil expressions it will hinder its ability to understand."*

> *"The more someone departs from evil, the more understanding he/she will have."*

Once the soul accepts the reality of evil, then it can grasp the reasonableness of behaviors, environments and conditions that affect human life. As a soul grasps the reasonableness of things, the soul becomes enabled to justly evaluate things or activities in life's value and nature. Another effect that will occur once a soul departs from evil is that it will endow the soul with the ability to interact around *opinions*. This effect will allow the soul to become tolerant in attitude, which will allow more peace to reign in its daily affairs.

**The effects of not having understanding:**

**Job 12:3**

**But I have understanding as well as you; I am not inferior to you:**

When a soul is absent of understanding, it will experience many shortcomings in the areas where the soul is deficient of understanding. Without a soul having an understanding, an individual will function below his/her true value or self-worth. Therefore, an individual will accept conditions or realities that don't measure with his/her true value or self-worth, because of the lack of understanding. A soul without understanding becomes submissive to environments, conditions and ideologies that do not elevate the well being of one's soul. This simply indicates that when a soul becomes submissive, an individual will lack the abilities to dominate his/her environment, being able to change their condition, being able to produce new ideologies, or being able to utilize existing ideologies to empower yourself or to empower others. Having a lack of mental or moral fitness is a result of a soul lacking understanding. In other words, the lack of mental or moral fitness refers to an individual being disabled to rule his/her spirit. As individuals lack understanding, it will cause them to be deprived of strength, vigor and spiritual intervention.

*"A soul that lacks understanding will function below his/her true value or self-worth."*

*"When an individual is absent of understanding, he/she will be deprived of spiritual empowerment."*

**The benefits of understanding:**

**Proverbs 19:8**
> He that keepeth understanding shall find good.

**Proverbs 16:22**
> Understanding is a wellspring of life unto him that hath it:

When an individual has understanding, he/she will be empowered to bring order and uniformity to their habits and behaviors. Having understanding allows an individual to be able to make corrections or adjustments from realities that will cause you to be destabilized in life. Understanding enables an individual to be able to restore his/her relationships back into harmony. As an individual has understanding, he or she is able to elevate spiritually, psychologically, socially and economically.

Another benefit of understanding is that it functions as a *wellspring* to those that have understanding. Wellspring refers to a source of continual supply of spiritual utilities that is able to enhance your well being. Spiritual utility refers to knowledge, wisdom, peace, love, courage, faith, patience, joy, creativity and anything that is intangible that can enhance your well being. To further expound, when someone has divine understanding, he/she have access to receive a continual supply of spiritual knowledge, spiritual wisdom, peace, love, courage, faith, patience, joy, creativity and et cetera. When an individual has access to a continual supply of spiritual utilities, he/she will be able to develop solutions to advance or change his/her environment, circumstance or condition. Understanding endows a soul with the ability to utilize and effectively benefit from a resource, skill, knowledge and relationships that he/she has access to. Along with this commentary of understanding, it can be concluded that when an individual, community or society has understanding, he/she can become progressive spiritually, socially and economically.

*"When an individual has access to understanding, he/she will become progressive spiritually, socially and economically."*

*"When someone lacks understanding, they will always be subject to his/her conditions."*

*"Understanding empowers you to change your condition."*

# Chapter 6
# "Changing Your Reality with the Environment"

**Proverbs 27:17**
**Iron sharpeneth iron; so a man sharpeneth the countenance of his friend.**

This principle presents how an environment evolves. Environment evolves according to how individuals sharpen the countenance of their friends or fellow community members. An environment is the aggregate of social and cultural conditions that influence the life of an individual or community. The activities of souls interacting refer to the term environment. Developing or forming cooperative and interdependent relationships also defines an environment.

Culture is an organized or a customary self-expression and collective behavior. The accumulation of values, knowledge, insights, beliefs, customs, principles and concepts (refers to a community educational standards and social responsibilities) that a community uses to function within society that is transferred or recycled generationally is culture, which makes up an environment. Culture includes the degree of acceptable behavior that a community approves to be expressed within society. All of these descriptive definitions of culture also define an environment because culture is an environment.

Therefore, environments are developed or created through individuals associating with one another for a mutual benefit, whether it may be beneficial or non-beneficial for the well being of an individual. Educational realities, domestic realities, customary beliefs, repetitive conduct or character, mindset and shared attitudes establish an environment. The state of the environment affects and influences the spiritual, psychological, moral and social well being, or fabric, of an individual or community. Environments affect someone reality because the consciousness of individual is molded according to how he/she interpret his/her experiences socially. This ultimately determines the psychological state as well as the moral standards that an individual or a community will personify.

*"Environments reflect individuals' or communities' educational realities, domestic realities, customary beliefs, repetitive conduct or character, mindset and shared attitudes."*

Remember, the aggregate of social conditions is an environment, and when the text states, *"so a man sharpeneth the countenance of his friends"* explains that an environment evolves according to how individuals behave towards each other. Every individual has influence and how someone uses his/her influence determines what shall be revealed within the environment, which refers to the mindsets, attitudes, word cycles, opinions, and displayed character of an individual or individuals.

An environment emerges when two or more individuals exchange their opinions, mindsets, attitudes and displayed character with one another. From this activity, an environment receives its labeling. For instance, when someone observes a group or a community operating collectively, socially, economically and politically, it would be labeled as being a communal-oriented group. Environments receive their label from people observing the displayed characters, word cycles, opinions, mindsets and shared attitudes that support the labeling of that environment.

In sum, individuals indoctrinate one another and the outcome of the indoctrinating activities creates the environment. Since each individual has influence, he/she willingly or unwillingly imbue those he/she influence with his/her opinions, point of views and principles of conduct. But the materialization or externalization of an individual influence is dependent on if the influenced individual accepts, assimilate or yield himself/herself to the influence of the influencing individuals.

Each individual possesses power to cause a social effect through an indirect or intangible way. Through the usage of this power, an individual consciously or unconsciously is able to win the devotion or allegiance of individuals through the activity of compelling an acceptance of your opinions, points of view, and principles of conduct. An example of using power through an indirect or intangible way is by being able to shift someone's *"ideas"* through using instruments such as educational institutions, radio, television and computers. These four instruments are powerful because they convey principles, ideologies and messages repetitively, which means someone *"ideas"* can become consumed by an individual consistently entertaining these *"ideas"* through these instruments. Therefore, environments are significant in changing your reality because it develops, breeds, creates, cultivates and sustains a certain *"mental image"* through the means of auditory and visual influences.

**Proverbs 14:7**

**Go from the presence of a foolish man, when thou perceivest not in him the lips of knowledge.**

**Proverbs 16:24**

**Pleasant words are as an honeycomb, sweet to the soul, and health to the bones.**

**I Corinthians 15:33**

**Be not deceived: evil communications corrupt good manners.**

In reference to these principles, the expressions *"evil communication"*, *"go from the presence of a foolish man"* and *"lips of knowledge or words"* all influence the environment. According to the Greek term *"homilia"*, communication refers to associations. The term *"presence"* that is in the phrase *"go from the presence of a foolish man"* refers to a demonstrated character. *"Lips of knowledge or words"* represent word cycles.

Therefore, the elements within the environment that influence your mental image are associations, demonstrated characters and word cycles.

Association is the process of forming mental or spiritual connections. Demonstrated character refers to the consistent displayed personality and attitude or mindset that you represent or project. Word cycles refer to the consistent ideas, opinions, motives, feelings or any ideology that is vocally transmitted among two or more individuals.

Mental or spiritual connection becomes developed according to emotional responses toward interests or feelings that individuals have in common. For clarification, mental or spiritual connections are developed accordingly due partly from the spiritual, psychological and physical responses marked by joy, pleasure, pain, attraction or repulsion that two or more individuals have in common. Individuals' formulated thoughts, opinions and beliefs foster a commonality for individuals to develop mental connections. The past experiences or a commonality of past experiences develop mental connections among individuals.

In reference to the spiritual principle *"evil communication corrupts good manners"* provides insights that pertain to associations. Activities or conditions that demote someone self worth or value is evil. Evil is to harm someone reputation through libel or slander. Depriving someone human qualities or to inhibit an individual to express his/her potential is evil. Therefore, anyone that develops mental or spiritual connections that exemplify evil will cause decay or ruin to behaviors and characters that are classified morally good or righteous.

Demonstrated character serves an importance concerning the environment because a *"character reproduces after itself"*. Within the statement *"go from the presence of a foolish man"* encourages an understanding that whatever character consistently surrounds someone will allow that person surrounded to personify or exhibit that consistent character that he/she are around. Each individual possesses the power to alter other's character or personality through the character they demonstrate. This is why it is imperative that the environment is important to change your reality through a demonstrated character and is why individuals become indoctrinated by someone's character. To further expound, if an individual is exposed or surrounded by a consistent character, he/she will become indoctrinated willingly or unwillingly. Therefore, the dominant character among homes, groups, communities or societies reflects the consistent character among them.

*"Character reproduces after itself."*

*"Individuals reflect the consistent character they are surrounded by."*

The environment is based on the word cycles or word patterns that circulate within it. Word cycles serve as importance concerning the environment because word cycles determine what someone's thought, ideas and mindset will be or become. A word is the spirit and soul of an individual that is vocally transmitted. Within every word, there is a social trait. In reference to every word, there is a social trait that indicates that words determine how souls will interact.

The reason why words determine how souls interact is because words construct or mold someone's character. Since no one acts independently from his/her character, individuals act out the words that they have yielded to. To further expound on the thought that *"within every word there is a social trait"* reveals how powerful a word is and how it relates to the environment. When an individual or individuals assimilate or cooperate with an image of a word, it will cause one's mindset to become the image of that word. As an individual becomes the image of a word, he/she will attract to anything similar to the image that resides in his/her mind.

Therefore, an environment influences one's reality because a word creates an image that engineers an individual or individuals into a solidified mindset and philosophy of living, which involves one's spiritual, social and economic standards or conduct. This solidification process affects this because a word produces an image, which motivates individuals who share the same image to draw toward that shared image. What this simply means is that an environment contains an image and because individuals draw toward the same image *"within them"*, they are actually drawing toward themselves. In reference to the previous sentence, it can be concluded that, *"our relationships is us"*. Wherefore, individuals can become accustomed to existing or new environments because word cycles within the environment can alter or indoctrinate the spirit, attitude, mindset, behavior and will of an individual. The reason why environments are important for changing one's reality is because of the *"meme effect"* within it. A *"meme effect"* is the activity of ideas, behaviors, customs or word cycles that spread from person to person within a culture or an environment. This is why the environment is an important element for changing your reality.

*"Our relationships is us."*

# Chapter 7
## "Reconditioning the Heart"

**Proverbs 4:23**
>    **Keep thy heart with all diligence: for out of it are the issues of life.**

Someone's reality changes when his/her heart changes. The state of the heart determines the activities that will occur in life. Along with that understanding, one can state that the heart determines and influences the state of our environments, societies and communities. Therefore, if someone desires to change his/her reality, they must be willing to adopt or become molded into a knowledge, wisdom, understanding and an environment that can assist him/her to express a different perspective and behavior along with allowing him/her to view life or life in general differently.

*"The state of the heart determines the activities that will occur in life."*

*"The heart determines and influences the state of our environments, societies and communities."*

The heart is the spiritual (non-physical) aspect of a person and this spiritual aspect is comprised from the spirit and soul revealing itself through the heart. Wherefore, the heart can be referred as the reflection of the spirit and soul. Therefore, someone is able to understand the state or condition of someone's spirit and soul through recognizing what is portrayed from his/her heart. This means the heart represents the soul and spirit.

According to Proverbs 4:23, the heart represents itself through its social and spiritual appetites along with what it produces during its course of life. In the book of Hebrews 10:22, the heart represents itself through its conscience or character. Viewing the book of Proverbs 23:7, the heart represents itself through the thought process or mindset. Examining Hebrews 4:12, the heart represents itself through its motives or intentions. Heeding John 14:27, the heart represents itself through its emotional responses to life situations and circumstances. Therefore, to summarize this paragraph, the heart reveals itself namely through:

- Its social and spiritual appetites
- What is produced during the course of someone lifetime
- Its conscience and character
- Its thought process and mindset
- Its motive and intentions
- Its emotional responses to life situations and circumstances.

To further expound, there are two definitions of the heart that comes from a Hebrew word *"me'ah"* and from a Greek word *"psuche"*. *"Me'ah"* means the seat of a generation. *"Psuche"* means vitality. The heart being a *"seat of a generation"* refers to the source and foundation of an individual personality, attitude, social appetite and character make-up is within his/her ancestry line. An example of this is when you witness certain families with a lot of educators throughout their ancestry. Vitality means the capacity to develop, which reveals the ability that the heart has. Having the capacity to develop means the heart can be changed or conditioned. Since the heart is changeable, the heart can always be reconditioned from what it is conditioned into.

Understanding the heart up to this point, it can be stated that the condition of the heart determines what a generation will continually express within their lively activities. Along with this statement, it can be stated that a generation course of life can be altered when the predecessor's heart has been changed. This simply furthers the understanding to state that the heart is where the history and potential of an individual resides. Since the heart is where one history and potential resides, it supports the understanding that the heart is hereditarily imparted or induced into us. This means what individuals produce in their lives are in correlation with what is inherently within their hearts.

*"To know someone's heart is to know the genesis of their behavior and mindset."*

Re-examining Proverbs 4:23 reveals that from out of the heart are the issues of life. The term *"issue"* refers to the social structures or contexts, environmental settings, conditions, or circumstances that society projects, or develops. *"Life"* refers to sensuality, personalities, and the state of the soul. The present state of existence, means of livelihood and the dominant attitudes among individuals, communities and society also refers to life. Therefore, life can be defined as the expression of heart. Along with this statement, you can revisit this definition and understand that life changes as the heart changes.

*"Life is the expression of the heart."*
*"Life changes as the heart changes."*

**Proverbs 23:7**
    **For as he thinketh in his heart, so is he:**

Viewing this principle, we can understand that the basis for reconditioning the heart begins with changing the thinking. This correlates how the heart affects the reality (perception) internally and externally. One's thinking programs his/her heart, which affects an individual internally. As this process continues, it is expressed externally (so is he). Therefore, changing the thinking is the center of focus concerning reconditioning the heart.

A thought is an idea or pattern of ideas, the process of turning something into the mind by the process of arranging ideas into a consistent pattern. Thinking is the power of reasoning, conceiving ideas and having the ability to form ideas and mental images. Thinking is an established belief system, words, opinions, values, perspective and principles that circulate within the mind. A thought serves as a blueprint for what a person plans to achieve or express in his/her life. What is expressed in life is a reflection of the thought. The thing we recognize in our thinking determines what we will energize and the thing that motivate and are active within us determine what we will realize in our life experiences.

In order for the heart to be reconditioned, your thoughts must conform to wisdom, knowledge, understanding and an environment that is contrary from your present reality (meaning to *discover your desired reality* and then align yourself with that reality knowledge base, wisdom base, understanding base, and environmental base). Thoughts conform to wisdom, knowledge, understanding and an environment through seeing, hearing and from receiving revelation or inspiration through the Spirit (John 16:13). As the thought is influenced by wisdom, knowledge, understanding, and environment, the heart will change, which will cause what an individual expresses in life to change. Therefore, all the principles within this book will contribute to your personal refinement.

*"Wisdom, knowledge, understanding, and the environment is the foundation for personal refinement."*

*Wisdom & Vibe Brand* is a brand that simply represents and reflects Gerald Seals message of community and spirituality. The motto, *"Developing Your Life with Wisdom"* simply articulates the intention of this brand, which is to help people work out possibilities in their life through wisdom. During the past 10 years is exactly what Gerald Seals has been doing on a grass root level. Throughout this 10 year period Gerald has developed a reputation for mending relationships, giving thought provoking spiritual teachings such as advocating self-improvement, building strong homes & families, positioning children for success, economic empowerment, community improvement, entrepreneurship, building & passing on wealth, diversity, social harmony, political awareness, pursuing education & embracing intellectuality.

Many describe Gerald Seals as a person with **wisdom** with the ability to create change. Due to people perceiving Gerald as **wisdom** along with creating change due to his wisdom points to Gerald **vibe**. That is why *Wisdom & Vibe Brand* is simply described as Gerald Seals. *Wisdom & Vibe Brand* is the vehicle Gerald uses to encourage spiritual enrichment, community upliftment, economic empowerment, self-improvement, social empowerment, practicing universal principles, communalism, and et cetera. *Wisdom & Vibe Brand* was developed for people encompassing all walks of life that desire to maximize their God given potential. The support from many people has allowed *Wisdom & Vibe Brand* to exist, which is represented by Gerald Seals.

The message of *Wisdom & Vibe Brand* is facilitated through books, eBooks, on-line activities, symposiums, conferences, spoken word CD's and other products. In addition to *Wisdom & Vibe Brand*, Gerald Seals is currently in the process of organizing a spiritual community that networks home-to-home through practicing the communal philosophy. All the core principles *Wisdom & Vibe Brand* advocates will serve as the foundation of this organization. This nonprofit organization is called the *Ruwach Communal Coalition*. This organization will give an individual a community that practices loving God, loving yourself, and loving your community within a communal structure. Therefore, the *Ruwach Communal Coalition* will be the body for *Wisdom & Vibe Brand* ideas.

Wisdom and Vibe Brand products is Distributed by Empowering Life International.

# About the Author

Gerald Seals II is a leader, spiritual teacher, business administrator, and communal activist. He is known for his spiritual wisdom for everyday issues, in-depth thinking, insight, teachings, and faith. His perspectives are clearly spiritually based, which cut across religious, political, cultural, and ethnic lines. Gerald is definitely an arising spiritual thinker for this next generation. His works has availed himself for speaking engagements at faith-based groups, church groups, college groups, community groups & grass root undertakings such as Ruwach Communal Coalition. Gerald has embraced the call toward maximizing human potential, empowerment, transformation, and community. Despite his personal accomplishments Gerald's greatest achievement is his relationship with his wife Latrease, in which they share two children Gerald Seals III and Shalom Seals.

Author Contact
www.gseals.net
Email: wisdomandvibe@att.net

# Empowering Life International Publishing and Distribution

Empowering Life Publishing, a full-service, self-publishing company providing authors a unique, and lucrative, alternative to traditional publishing. While maintaining 100% of all publishing rights and profits, new-generational authors are given the independence and option to be involved in as much or as little of the decision making

Empowering Life Publishing
changing the world through books

and creative process as desired. We help custom design, produce, and self-publish your book to fit your needs.

We represent the innovative leader in the book publishing industry. Our clients receive professional and personal, one-on-one, attention generally not afforded authors associated with traditional publishing houses. Empowering Life International makes publishing fast, easy and affordable for today's author. Empowering Life International has helped authors with books that have not been accepted by traditional presses. Our technology allows you to get your book into print quickly, while distributing through Ingram and making it available for sale as well as achieving high sales ranks with the world's leading booksellers:

- ○ *Barnes and Noble.com*
- ○ *Amazon.com*
- ○ *Booksamillion.com*
- ○ *Buy.com*
- ○ *and many, many more*

By choosing Empowering Life International as your book publisher, you join a rapidly growing and innovative group of author-entrepreneurs who elect to take control of their own project. We offer professional self publishing services that include the formatting of your book for publication; interior page layout, book cover design, copyediting, indexing and advanced marketing tools like website design. These services are individually priced, and you can choose to use them or not at your own discretion or level of publishing experience. Our layout, design and formatting process is fastest among book publishing companies. In most cases, you're book could be published in 3 months.

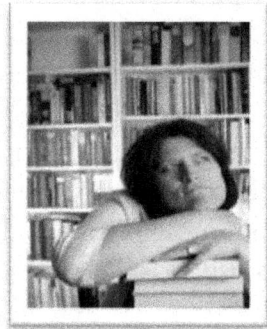

When you do the math and compare, Empowering Life International clearly stands apart from the crowd as a publishing company. Whether your book is a novel, poetry book, memoir or technical manual, we place your interests first.

If you have a story to share and if your dream is to write and publish your story in book form, don't hesitate to contact us at info@empoweringlifeinternational.com.

# Attention Vendors

Any person, business, organization or group can become a distributor or a facilitator of our materials. By simply purchasing a minimum number (10) of books or compact disks, a distributor is entitled to the wholesale rate. The discount for our products varies according to the specific products. We welcome anyone who desires to join us in pushing for the development of enlightenment, creativity, social consciousness and a safe world.

## Distribution Membership Benefits
- *Newsletters*
- *Economic Opportunities*
- *Sample Products*
- *Promotional Pre-Released Books (PDF)*
- *Networking Events*
- *Entrepreneurial Opportunities*

## Distribution Membership Requirements
- *Application on File*
- *Purchase at least $100.00 worth of products per quarter (3 months period).*

# Become a Facilitator

If you have been changed by our books become an Empowering Life Facilitator. This is a weekend-long intensive program designed to provide you with the skills you need to create powerful, transformative workshops. Empowering Life Facilitator training is designed by CEO and the Signature authors of Empowering Life, This training will provide you with the tools you need to enhance your confidence, create new depth to your presentations,

During the course of the weekend, you will learn how to facilitate the some of the foundational books the Empowering Life Company. You will learn how to:

1. *Create and engaging environment that stimulate discussion.*
2. *Lead session that that will leave your participants feeling touched, open, valued and nurtured.*
3. *Generate an environment where women and men communicate more authentically.*
4. *Listen profoundly*

5.  *Create a powerful relatedness with strangers quickly and easily.*
6.  *Be more open to others and able to give and receive comfortably.*
7.  *Create strong boundaries for yourself without shutting others down.*

You will also learn:

   *\* Business Skills that can be used to sell each of the products while also making your own business.*
   *\* How to use the Advertisement Tool Kit to Generate Sales or Host Coach Talk Parties*
   *\* How to set-up a Successful Empowering Life Facilitator Coaching Business.*
   *\* Much More*

For more information about this wonderful opportunity, don't hesitate to contact us at info@empoweringlifeinternational.com.

www.ingramcontent.com/pod-product-compliance
Lightning Source LLC
LaVergne TN
LVHW051204080426
835508LV00021B/2793